# Sprite At Night

© 2013 by JOAN FERGUSON
ALL RIGHTS RESERVED.

No part of this publication may be reproduced, distributed or transmitted in any form or by any means, including photocopying, recording, or other electronic or mechanical methods, without the prior written permission of the author, except in the case of brief quotations or reproductions of illustrations embodied in critical reviews and certain other noncommercial uses permitted by copyright law.

Permission requests should be submitted to daisydog@sonic.net.

Special discounts are available on quantity purchases by schools, associations, corporations, and others. For details, contact daisydog@sonic.net.

PALO ALTO PUBLISHING
3340 St. Michael Dr.
Palo Alto, CA 94306

BOOK DESIGN AND PRODUCTION: Amparo del Rio
EDITORIAL CONSULTANT: Holly Brady

Printed in the U.S.A., by AMP Printing & Graphics: www.ampprinting.com

First printing, 2013
ISBN-13: 978-0-9839398-5-6

# Sprite At Night

## A Deer Hollow Farm Story

BY JOAN FERGUSON

ILLUSTRATED BY CLARE DeZUTTI

Palo Alto Publishing

The barn is getting dark,
and the first stars sparkle in the sky.
Sprite, the farm cat,
wakes up with a big stretch.
Time to check on all the animals.

Luna, the cow, and her calf
walk slowly to their barn on the hill.
No more mooing.
No more sneaking apples from
the tree.

Each mama goat
gathers her baby kids.
They sleep in a soft bed of
straw for the night.

Shhh...it's quiet in the chicken coop.
No more dusty scratching
in the dirt.
No more crowing.

Olive, the mama pig,
and her piglets
snuggle up into a cozy pile.

There they are...Maggie, Muffin, and Peter.

The rabbits sleep very close together, so they feel safe and warm.
No more hopping through the chicken yard to look for treats.

All of the sheep curl up and rest their furry heads.

No more chewing alfalfa.

Watch over us, Owl,
my night time friend.

All is peaceful at the farm.

Goodnight, Sprite.

JOAN FERGUSON has been a docent and animal care volunteer at Deer Hollow Farm since 2008. She lives in Redwood City, California. She is grateful to Farmer Jen, Julie and Evan for patiently teaching a city girl how to work with farm animals. And, of course, she thanks Jess, Jacquie, Jaime, and Claire.

CLARE DeZUTTI is an illustrator currently working in Baltimore and San Francisco. She likes playing with the baby goats and finding Sprite when he hides in the barn. She would like to thank Joan Ferguson and the farm volunteers.